NOW OR NEVER

UNLOCKING YOUR POTENTIAL FOR SUCCESS AND GROWTH

SHRAVAN NARAYAN

To every young dreamer who has been told, "You're too young to succeed." This book is for you—because your youth is your greatest strength. Keep pushing boundaries, breaking limits, and proving the world wrong.

Contents

Foreword

The world is changing, and young minds like Shravan Narayan are at the forefront of this transformation. His journey from a 16-year-old entrepreneur to a successful founder, mentor, and innovator is nothing short of inspiring.

This book isn't just a collection of ideas—it's a roadmap. Shravan has distilled his experiences into practical, actionable strategies that any teenager can apply to kickstart their entrepreneurial journey. Whether you're looking to build a startup, create content, or make an impact, Now or Never will equip you with the mindset and tools to start today.

I wish I had a book like this when I was younger. Now, you do.

Preface

I was 16 when I decided to break the mold. While my peers focused solely on academics, I was launching Code Cave, balancing school and business, and proving that age is just a number.

I wrote this book because I know what it feels like to doubt yourself. To wonder if you're "too young," "too inexperienced," or "not ready." But here's the truth—your youth is your greatest advantage. You have time, energy, and creativity on your side. The world is evolving, and there's never been a better time to take action.

This book is not just about motivation—it's about execution. Each chapter gives you actionable steps, real-world examples, and challenges to push you forward. The goal? To turn your ideas into reality before you even graduate.

If you've been waiting for the perfect time, Now or Never is your answer.

Acknowledgements

No journey is ever truly solo, and mine is no exception.

A heartfelt thank you to my family for believing in my vision, even when it seemed unconventional. To my mentors at Talrop and Steyp, who guided me and fueled my passion for technology and entrepreneurship.

To my team at Code Cave—you are the backbone of everything we've built together. And to every teacher, friend, and supporter who encouraged me along the way—this book exists because of your belief in me.

Finally, to the readers of Now or Never—thank you for taking this leap with me. Your dreams matter, and I can't wait to see what you create.

Prologue

Imagine this—you're sitting in class, staring out the window, daydreaming about a future that seems just out of reach. Maybe you want to start a business, create content, or build something extraordinary, but a voice in your head keeps whispering: "Not yet."

That voice is lying.

I started my entrepreneurial journey with nothing but an idea and a laptop. Today, I run a successful tech company, mentor startups, and speak to thousands of students. And the best part? I'm still just getting started.

This book is about rewriting the rules. It's about proving that you don't need to wait until you're older to chase your dreams. You have everything you need right now—ambition, curiosity, and the internet.

So let's dive in. The time is Now or Never.

CHAPTER ONE

INTRODUCTION

Do you know the fact that most of today's successful entrepreneurs were right there starting from being a teenager? Mark Zuckerberg founded Facebook from his college dorm room, and Bill Gates was programming at age 13. Their stories show that age doesn't matter if you strive for the thing you want in life.

In "Now or Never," you will learn why these are the ideal launch years for your dreams. Here, this book explodes the myth that success happens only at the end by showing ways in which youth can be your best asset: time, energy, and the freedom to experiment without the burdens that accompany life later on.

What makes this guide so unique is its very practical and teen-centric approach. Instead of boring, generic business advice, every chapter deals with how to address the unique challenges of being a young entrepreneur-from balancing schoolwork with business ventures to getting parents and peers to take your dreams seriously. The book combines real-life case studies, actionable strategies, and step-by-step guidance tailored exclusively for teenage go-getters.

Three common threads run through all of this: acting sooner rather than later, using failure as a learning experience for success, and how to create helping networks. What does this mean? Whether you dream of launching a startup, mastering a creative skill, or making a difference in your community, this book provides the roadmap to turn your ideas into reality while navigating the turbulence of adolescence.

Addressed to ambitious young adults who refuse to wait for "someday," this book will speak directly to those who sense they're capable of more but aren't sure where to start. By the final page, you'll have the tools, confidence, and clarity to take those crucial first steps toward your dreams - because the time to start is now.

CHAPTER TWO

STARTING EARLY: THE POWER OF BEGINNING NOW

Countless exceptionally bright young minds have been hindered by the usual perception that success and achievement can only result from age. For myself, who started a successful tech company from my bedroom as a sixteen-year-old, I know that age is just a number when it comes to striving after dreams. The fact that teens should spend their prime academic years and delay their aspirations is not only a quaint notion but also an approach that could stop one's development and potential for later success.

Think of Mark Zuckerberg, who began coding when he was still a middle schooler, and at college, founded Facebook. Then there is Moziah Bridges, who founded Mo's Bows- his bow tie company when he was just nine years old-so much is possible if young people put their ideas to the test instead of holding out for the right time in the future.

Research has now always proved that the adolescent brain is indeed wired for innovation and creative thinking. According to a leading neuroscientist at University College London, Dr. Sarah-Jayne Blakemore, "The adolescent brain has heightened plasticity, an ideal time for learning and creativity." It's this biological advantage, coupled with relative freedom from adult responsibilities, for which so few people prepare themselves for. It's in these early years that the neural pathways formed will adapt the pathways for future success. Thus, while it is important to take action early, by doing so, it may be the most effective to gain lasting success.

Fear may hide behind the illusion of "waiting for the right moment." Most teenagers I have coached complain about not being resourceful or not having experience but both can be advantages. Younger entrepreneurs are exempted from the weight of other settled routines and set minds. They are unshackled and free to assess their problems afresh with open-ended novel options. As said by Richard Branson, "If somebody offers you an amazing opportunity but you are not sure you can do it, say yes – then learn how to do it later."

Never in human history has there been such democratization of access to knowledge and resources as in the digital age. Today's teenagers have access to information databases of volumes and scope that entire universities had mere decades ago. Online learning platforms, social media networks, and collaborative tools have virtually eliminated the barriers of entry that once existed. The playing field has leveled out in ways that make early starts not just possible but even advantageous.

Time management becomes the necessary skill when balancing academic responsibilities with entrepreneurial pursuits. However, this juggling act teaches valuable lessons in prioritization and efficiency that really prove invaluable later in life. Many successful young entrepreneurs report that their ventures actually improved academic performance by teaching them better organization and focus. The key is to see one thing and not the other as priorities.

Long gone is the idea that to start a venture requires one to have an enormous amount of initial capital for such an endeavor. Many of today's successful ventures began with very small investment, creativity, and a little hustle between them. Just consider Cameron Johnson, who started his first business when he was nine years old, by designing greeting cards on his computer. By the time he was fifteen, he was earning thousands of dollars monthly from various online ventures. Initial investment was minimal; the return was substantial.

The other important advantage to the early starter is early networking: because teens can start building up a support network long before adults have had a chance to establish serious professional networks, they are way ahead on these when they get into the workforce. School connections, social media, and community resources can serve as fertile grounds for young people to build their support systems from scratch.

These early experiences in networking often ring truer and last longer than those formed at older ages. "Failure" has a new flavor of meaning when you're young. No mortgages, no families to support, means that teens can play around and make mistakes without having the whole world come crashing down on their heads. Freedom to fail and switch gears quickly is something most of the world is getting less and less of as the years go by. As Thomas Edison quipped when he failed somewhere in the neighborhood of 10,000 times trying to invent the light bulb, "I have not failed. I've just found 10,000 ways that won't work."

When you are young, understanding the dynamics of the market and people's behavior becomes second nature. Taking it at a teenage perspective offers unique insights into emerging trends and youth markets, which most adult entrepreneurs cannot seem to catch. It is only natural that a very high value for such knowledge in developing products or services set to resonate with young consumers will be accrued.

If you start early, you can focus on organic growth instead of pushing a concept that may not yet be ready for the market. You don't have to try to be an overnight success. You can experiment, iterate, and evolve your ideas in their natural path. In this organic way of working, you end up with more sustainable and authentic success than forcing something into the market that it may not be ready for.

Skills achieved through early entrepreneurship are much more than business acumen. Problem-solving, communication, leadership, and resilience are skills that any future path-trail will carry into business, academics, or whatever the person chooses. Soft skills, which are so grossly absent in traditional education, become part of second nature if learned in the real world.

As you continue on to the working application of goal-setting and overcoming initial stumbling blocks, remember that your best asset is youth itself. The energy, malleability, and fresh viewpoint that you have today is an ability too valuable to squander away by waiting for the "better time" to get started. The next chapter will show you step-by-step how to build you

Building Your Roadmap - Goal Setting and Visioning

As we explore in "Building Your Roadmap," this is a key step in most travelers' journey toward their dreams: goal setting and vision crafting. As a teenager, you probably have various interests and dreams of what you would like to do. Defining goals can provide you with direction and purpose in life and, consequently, motivate you.

1. Your 'Why

Before setting any goals, first understand the "why" of your dreams. Reflect with me on what fuels you: creativity, desire to help others, a new creation, a dream home, a healthier state, or something else. Make sure you get to the bottom of what drives you, as that will fuel your journey and ground you as you hit bumps in the road.

2. Breaking Down Your Big Dream into Smaller Goals

Big dreams are impressive but generally too large to be achieved. However, breaking these big dreams into steps makes it quite feasible. This section helps you in the process of breaking down a big goal, like starting up a business or learning a new language, into some actual steps. For instance, if you plan to start a small business, one possible first step is researching the market, devising a brand name, and actually working out a plan for the first product. Each of these miniature steps takes you closer to what you want.

3. SMART Goal Setting

In the chapter, we are going to offer you to become aware of SMART goals (Specific, Measurable, Achievable, Relevant, Time-Bound). You will learn how to formulate your aspirations in concrete terms with the help of SMART goals. The current chapter includes examples about writing SMART goals concerning the type of projects-for example, growing a social media following, achieving academic targets, or beginning some creative project. It means that now you can make your progress measurable and tangible.

4. Vision Boards and Planning for the Future

Create a vision board. In this lesson, you will be instructed on how to create an electronic or paper vision board that represents your dreams, goals, and inspiration. It will then explain the magic of visualization in keeping you positive and focused on your future.

5. Being Adaptive and Responsive to Change

Goals can change as you do. This chapter asks you to become fluid and change your goals as circumstances change and as you meet new challenges and opportunities. The experiences of young entrepreneurs who adjusted their goals along the way help demonstrate that it's okay to switch directions if it feels right for you.

6. How to Set Milestones and Celebrate Success

It's a marathon, not a sprint. This section emphasizes that there should be milestones or small victories along the way. You also have time to celebrate them. Celebrating just how little keeps you motivated and reminds you that every step counts.

7. Action and Moving On

The chapter ends with instructions on action, how to start the transition from planning into action. This is more on the beginning, rather than planning itself it is the most important thing to start.

You don't require a perfect plan to start; what counts is that first step.

Chapter Summary:

In "Building Your Roadmap," you will find a fundamental, no-fuss primer in the art of goal-setting and planning that's essential to any success, together with the tools to set clear goals, understand your motivations for what you want to achieve, and map out the picture of the road ahead for you. If you take action on each of these steps, you will lay down a strong foundation for turning your dreams into reality, so every day is a meaningful step forward.

CHAPTER FOUR

Overcoming Fears and Barriers

Chapter 4 is where we will face some fears and how to overcome them. The biggest barrier to achieving success is often the fear complex: fear of failure, fear of rejection, or not knowing where to start. Every teenager has doubts and barriers that come up when trying new things. This chapter incorporates tools and strategies for overcoming fears and the way forward in cultivating resilience and confidence.

1. Familiarity with Normative Anxieties This chapter deals with what kinds of anxieties an average young person encounters in the course of everyday life: anxiety over judgment, fear of failure, and even the dread of not being "good enough." Once you start to acknowledge these fears, you begin to understand that they are only part of an ordinary development and, therefore, should not restrict your progress. Personal examples and stories do help show how young entrepreneurs and creators have managed similar challenges.

2. Turn Failure Culture into Success Sometimes failure presents with the window of opportunity to be learned.

This section will have you approach failure not as a step backward but as a step forward. It teaches you the concept of a "growth mindset" where you view challenges and failures as opportunities for growth and development. Real examples, such as how J.K. Rowling's multiple rejections honed her craft, in many cases, perseverance pays off.

3. Creating a Network

Having a support system makes the hurdles easier to overcome. This chapter discusses how to find mentors, friends, and peers on the journey who would want to see your dreams become a reality. Tips on networking through school, online, and in the community guide readers through this very important factor of bringing positive energy into their lives to surround themselves with supportive people .

4. Taking Small, Brave Steps

Sometimes the only way to vanquish fear is to act, but action can be tiny and manageable. Chapter 5 lays so much weight on the "micro-actions," which are little steps toward your goals but very meaningful. If you fear public speaking, for example, you might begin speaking to small groups, or even practice alone. Every single small action puts you one step closer to more giant ambitions.

5. Dealing with Rejection and Criticism

Life will probably scorn and criticize you. This chapter shows you how to take medicinal doses of negative criticism instead of letting these detour your spirit. Instead, you learn on how to turn criticisms into strength and view rejections as redirection. Examples here include some of the most famous people in history who were stumped by setbacks but turned them into strengths, starting with the legendary one who cut Michael Jordan off from his high school basketball team.

6. Self Compassion and Positive Self Speaking

Positive inner voice control before fighting the battleground. In this chapter, the author teaches skills for self-compassion where you learn your mistakes are not who you are. Through learning positive self-speaking, you learn to replace discouraging self-talk with encouragement and this is when the difference in dealing with failures could be clearly identified.

7. Learning Resilience and the Journey

It means to bounce back in adversity. In the final portion of this chapter, you will learn how to develop persistence and flexibility to be able to bounce back and withstand the adversity life throws your way. Of course, life doesn't always go according to plan, but with resilience, you can adapt, learn, and move on. Here are some final stories of young people who faced hardship but continued to grow and eventually succeeded.

Chapter Summation "Walk Through Fears Overcome Obstacles." Understand you will never be without challenges in your life, the different strategies given regarding reframing failure, managing fear, and building resilience. Taking small steps, support from around you, and coming at obstacles with confidence and learning from every experience should make you grow stronger with every challenge overcome-giving you the drive and nerve to pursue your dreams relentlessly.

CHAPTER FIVE

TIME MANAGEMENT AND BALANCE

In Chapter 5, "Mastering Time Management and Balance," you learn how to balance your entrepreneurial endeavors with school, extracurricular activities, family time, and downtime. This chapter will illustrate that you can balance responsibilities while following your passions and yet maintain your well-being. You will be mastering a lifelong skill that you can apply in anything.

1. Setting Priorities: What Counts

This page teaches you how to identify and rank your priorities. You will learn techniques, like the "Eisenhower Matrix," to categorize tasks as urgent, important, or not that critical. This helps you determine which efforts to put forth every day and makes sure important academic and personal commitments aren't missed. Real-life examples show how other teens have used prioritization to do well on their studies and their ventures.

2. Create a schedule that works for you In this chapter, you will learn how to create an effective schedule that works for you. From digital planners to notebooks, learn the tools and techniques for planning your day and also how to blend structured routines with enough flexibility to absorb changes. See examples of sample schedules created by young entrepreneurs showing how to fit in study sessions, meetings, and other personal time.

3. The Art of Saying 'No'

Learn how to say "no". Time management skills are saying no just right. Learn how to politely decline invitations or commitments you truly cannot keep with your priorities. Setting boundaries and sometimes needing to say no to less important activities can be what increases productivity and decreases stress overload. Teens' stories about overcommitting help show how learning to say "no" helped them improve their progress.

4. Controlling distractions, and how to stay focused Distractions are one of the biggest productivity waste makers, especially with the pull of social media most of the time. This section will teach you how to minimize distractions and develop habits that will help you keep yourself on the track of focusing on things that must be done. It will teach techniques such as the Pomodoro Technique, working in focused intervals, followed by breaks, and how to put restrictions on apps. You will develop your ability to focus better, complete jobs much quicker, and much more effectively.

5. School-Business Balance: Time-Saving Hacks

Balancing a high school schedule with a side venture is pretty challenging, so this chapter introduces you to some specific time-saving hacks that really make it possible. From batched processing to digital tools like Trello and Notion, you'll know how to work smart in the sense of workflow. You will find out how to maximize "hidden" time-such as studying on your commute, or listening to audiobooks during chores-so that you become more productive without sacrificing relaxation or downtime.

6. Break Time and Fighting Burnout

Achieving balance also includes knowing when it's time to take a break. This chapter describes why breaks are part of mental and physical wellness, including how to make the most of your breaks throughout the day. Practices such as the "20-20-20 rule," where you take a 20-second break every 20 minutes to look at something 20 feet away, as well as power naps refresh your energy without letting your momentum slip. You will also learn signs of burnout and adjust when you are putting too much pressure on yourself .

7. Self-Reflecting and readjusting your strategy

Time management is not something that fits into a box, and what worked yesterday may need to change today. This chapter encourages you to evaluate your habits regularly and adjust them to better fit how you work or live. Regular evaluation of your schedule will let you know what works and what doesn't so that continuous improvement-how you manage your time-will be possible.

Summary of the Chapter

"Mastering Time Management and Balance" arms you with tools and strategies for effective balancing of the pursuits with school and personal life. It's made possible through prioritized, disciplined scheduling, as well as control over distractions to maximize usage of time available. Flexibility, self-care, and reflection serve as reminders to not get burnt out while being productive. It helps you make steady progress toward your goals. I will have the next chapter where you'll be provided with a personalized approach towards time management fitted for both your dreams and day-to-day responsibilities.

CHAPTER SIX

Becoming Able to Accept Failure as a Preface to Success

Chapter 6: Embracing Failure as a Stepping Stone to Success Challenging the notion of fear of failure is the reframing of it into something that has served a purpose for growth. Here you'll find how every setback helps you in learning and growing with greater strength and adjustment. Understand that the difference between success and failure is a step; and with that understanding, you'll face challenges with greater resilience in a healthier mind.

1. Redefining Failure: Why It's Not the End

In this section, why defeat is one of the important elements towards any eventual, final success is discussed. Read stories of failures-legendary failures by J.K. Rowling's publishers and hundreds of attempts by Thomas Edison before that light bulb finally worked. This way, the setbacks would turn out to be temporary and valuable compared to finals. Such success stories by early entrepreneurs who turned early mistakes as lessons show how failure becomes a stepping stone for future achievements.

Switching over to a Growth Mindset

Here, you'll get to know the "growth mindset," a new concept proposed by psychologist Carol Dweck. The growth mindset believes that the abilities and intelligences are in a growing cycle through dedication and efforts. You will then start seeing challenges as roads to growth rather than threats. I will also introduce several exercises to learn that you will practice to develop this mindset in your minds with a view towards failures that are desired only to improve.

3. Learning from Errors: Critical Analysis of Mistakes

Failures also teach valuable lessons and this chapter teaches you how to dissect what you could have done otherwise. You will learn how to take a step back and objectively analyze each failure, making visible factors that brought the result. This gives you an understanding of why things didn't work out, so you can take your chances another day. Live examples of teen entrepreneurs who learned from their failures and were able to tweak their product offers in such a manner that they were able to achieve success in practice.

4. Building Resilience: Bouncing Back Stronger

Resilience-the ability to bounce back from obstacles-is one factor that has much to do with success. Here you will learn methods to develop mental and emotional toughness, for example, holding multiple perspectives, practicing self-compassion, and using failure as a catalyst for motivation toward continued efforts. You will learn how to build a support network of friends, mentors, or peers who can help you stay the course in your time of need.

5. Using Failure as Fuel for Innovation

Sometimes, failure can be that spark that leads you to innovative solutions that you may never have considered otherwise. This chapter gives examples of innovations born out of failure: James Dyson's 5,000+ prototypes of the revolutionary Dyson vacuum. Learn to let failure be the fuel of creativity by looking out for alternatives and trying out new ideas instead of repeating the same thing.

6. Celebrating Small Wins Along the Way

Acknowledging tiny victories gives you a sense of momentum and keeping an optimistic mentality, even when disasters happen. This chapter enables you to celebrate, no matter how minute, to emphasize the feeling of success. The more each attempt is perceived as worth it, the less hurting failure will be, and progress seems doable.

7. Translating Failure to Fuel: Stepping Out with Confidence

It's a section that motivates you to burn each failure into fuel to propel you forward. Here, you learn to let your doubts work for you in driving you towards your goals instead of letting them be a fixation on what should have been done.

This chapter also spells out practical tips on how to maintain momentum after a failure as well as a long-term perspective on achieving success.

"Embracing Failure as a Stepping Stone to Success" is a transformative perspective in the way one thinks about failure: No longer something to fear but a precious tool in personal and professional improvement. With a growth mindset and resilience, you will learn how to analyze and adapt and improve from every setback. By the end of this chapter, you will understand how failure becomes part of the journey and how you will use it to fuel your ambitions instead of being held back by it. With these skills on your belt, challenges would be met head-on, knowing in real life that every step forward brings you one closer to success.

CHAPTER SEVEN

BUILDING YOUR SUPPORT SYSTEM AND NETWORK

Chapter 7, "Building Your Support System and Network," is where you will discover why the right network and supportive community will become one of your best assets toward your success. In this chapter, let's understand the value of connection to people who could be very helpful in the guidance they provide, sharing some resources, and keeping you motivated. At first glance, building a network may seem daunting, but with practical advice tailored to teenagers, you'll find it's really not that hard to get meaningful connections up and running.

1. Why You Need a Support System

Start with the importance of having people who believe in your potential and want to see you succeed. While work and resolve are requirements, the process can go much smoother with a network of supporters. Here, you'll find out just how mentors, friends, family, and other people within your community can advise you, encourage you, and give you critical support that can help get you closer to your goals more quickly. You will learn how other young entrepreneurs have found mentors, teachers, or local business owners who were critical to their own success.

2. Finding Key People: Mentors, Peers, and Role Models

Identify the right people to be part of your support system. This chapter breaks down the types of people-mentors, peers, and role models. Mentors can offer you wisdom and experience; peers bring collaboration and shared experiences; and role models help you want to aspire to achieve more. You'll learn to identify and reach out to others who may fulfill each of these roles in your life-take a teacher, a local business leader, an older student, or online communities.

Networking: Real Connections

Generally, people view networking as a skill attained by adults, but relationships can be built regardless of age. Learn practical skills to networking, from how to introduce yourself through a genuine show of interest and thoughtful questions. Techniques include using events in school, community groups, or even social media applications to further your network. This section also places value in relationships through non-selfishness support provided to others with an understanding of gaining that one wouldn't have gotten otherwise.

4. Leveraging Social Media to Scale

With social media, you have the ability to connect with people all over the world. You will learn how to use tools such as LinkedIn, Instagram, and Twitter to get beyond your immediate circle of people. You'll learn how to make those connections and even reach out professionally to share your goals, in order to find people who think similarly.

5. Seek Groups, Clubs, and Communities There are often clubs, organizations, or online forums at school and in the community that may be a source of belonging and support. This section describes how joining a group of people that share your interest helps you meet people who are just as passionate and ambitious. Maybe it is an entrepreneurial club, coding group, or community volunteer program-these groups often have interesting experiences, insights, and connections.

6. Overcoming fear of asking for help

Sometimes, fear of being rejected or looking clueless will scare people off from asking for help. In this chapter, you will learn how to get over those fears and realize that asking for help is a strength, not a weakness. You will get practical advice on how to reach out, ask the questions, and follow up professionally. Most of all, though, you'll realize most people like helping others, especially young people wanting to learn.

7. Networking and Paying It Forward A network is a two-way street: not just people who will give you something, but to whom you will pay forward. In the last chapter, you'll learn how to show your gratitude, keep in touch, and pay it forward to others in your network. You could do it by assisting someone else when they need it, being gracious enough to send a thank-you note, or helping others get to where you want to be. Networking is a mutually good business. In this lesson, you learned how to build a relationship.

Summary So far, this chapter has detailed the importance of building relationships and why networking is a good business.

"Building Your Support System and Network" shows you how you can marshal the support of a network of people who will be there for you on your journey and help you grow a supportive community. Identify key figures, learn networking skills, use social media strategically, and above all, give back to those who help you. With this chapter end, you will be prepared to find and create these links for sure, which would be of tremendous value on your travels.

CHAPTER EIGHT

TIME AND PRIORITIES MANAGEMENT

In Chapter 8, "Time and Priorities Management," you learn how to balance multiple commitments-a key skill for young entrepreneurs balancing school, activities, personal life, and business pursuits. Time management is at the core of successful entrepreneurship, and this chapter provides a step-by-step guide that helps you be organized, thereby eliminating extra anxiety in your life and making the most out of your time.

1. The Value of Time

This section begins with the concept that time is the most precious resource you have. Although you are a teen with far fewer responsibilities than adults, using your time intentionally can steer you toward long-term success. You'll explore the notion of an "opportunity cost" and how small, everyday decisions about how you spend your time add up to big outcomes over months and years.

2. How to set SMART Goals for Concentration: SMART is an acronym that describes the criteria for specific, measurable, achievable, relevant, and time-bound goals. You will learn how to break big goals down into smaller, easily manageable tasks that will keep you feeling motivated and allow you to track your progress.

See examples of how to apply SMART goals in real-life work-forces-whether reaching a certain grade or revenue target in a business-of young entrepreneurs.

Creating a Daily and Weekly Plan

A routine schedule is one of the easy ways to keep on top of things. Here, you will learn how to set up an effective daily and weekly plan of activities both academic and entrepreneurial. The section is supplemented with sample schedules and planning tools - digital or paper planners - in order to demonstrate to you how a combination of routine chores can contribute to greater productivity while allowing some flexibility.

4. The Power of the "80/20 Rule" (Pareto Principle)The Pareto Principle, or 80/20 Rule, suggests that 80% of your results come from 20% of your efforts. In this section, you will learn to identify highimpact tasks-the ones that forward your goals the most-and how to prioritize them and put less critical activities second. You will be guided on how to focus on those tasks that give you the most value in terms of results, maximizing your time and energy for important outcomes.

5. Productivity and Focus Management Learn how to identify sources of distraction such as excessive social media use or screen time, which are sucking up your energy and focus. You will learn techniques such as "batching," or completing a set of similar tasks together; the "Pomodoro Technique," focused work periods followed by breaks for maintaining the brain's concentration. Helpful tips on managing devices, integrativeness, and setting boundaries while keeping yourself on track.

6. Developing the Habit of Prioritization

Prioritizing is the skill that will allow you to decide what would be the most important to do for any given day. Here, you'll learn how to rate tasks by the level of urgency versus importance and by using the tool of the Eisenhower Matrix: a decision-making aid that graphically separates your activities into priorities on a scale of urgent vs. important. This habit will allow you to make concrete, confident decisions about where to place your time and attention.

7. Developing Resilience to Prevent Burnout

With all this on your plate, it is easy to become overwhelmed. This part shares guidelines for developing resilience by recognizing early signs of burnout and building techniques for stress management by observing regular breaks, exercises, and mindfulness. You will learn that sustainable productivity requires maintaining one's well being as well and taking time off to recharge.

8. Learning when to say no

Sometimes it is hard to learn how to say "no, especially for young entrepreneurs with the urge to prove themselves. Declining on unimportant tasks or social commitments that don't apply to their goals frees up what actually matters. The following section provides lessons on how to say no respectfully and how to arm oneself to make choices in support of priorities.

Summary Chapter:

"Mastering Time Management and Prioritization" gives tools to manage the demands of school, business, and personal life. Understanding time's value, setting SMART goals, creating realistic plans, and focusing on high-impact activities, all this should give control over the schedule. This lesson emphasizes that productivity is a matter of working smarter, not harder, allowing an individual to balance ambitions and responsibilities.

CHAPTER NINE

BUILDING A NETWORK AND FINDING MENTORS

In Chapter 9, "Building a Network and Finding Mentors," you will discover how the right relationships can spur your growth and success. Networking and mentorship are powerful tools that provide the support, advice, and opportunities needed to speed up your young entrepreneurial journey. This chapter reveals how to build effective relationships with your peers, mentors, and industry professionals-even as a teenager.

1. Why Networking Matters, Especially When You're Young Building a network early can provide access to resources, insights and collaborations that otherwise are not available to entrepreneurs. This chapter discusses why networking is so important for young entrepreneurs and which may be an open door to opportunities, acceleration of learning and emotional support from like-minded people who understand your journey.

2. How to Identify Potential Mentors

A right mentor is going to change the game for you, as he or she has lived it. At the end of the book, I will teach you how to find a mentor: that can be teachers and local business owners, up to online communities and family friends. You are going to learn what a good mentor is and why finding someone who's aligned with your goals and values is so important.

3. Reaching Out And Building Authentic Connections

It might be intimidating to approach someone you consider a potential mentor or professional. This section will give you tips on how to approach someone kindly and authentically, from developing an email to introducing yourself to reaching each other via social media. You'll learn how to genuinely take a real interest in their work and form mutually beneficial relationships.

4. Networking in a Digital World

Social media and professional networks such as LinkedIn, Twitter, and others make networking more accessible than ever. You'll learn how to use LinkedIn, Twitter, and other instruments for reaching experts, entrepreneurs, and young achievers across the world. This chapter will share with you how to expand your online network, including participating in online groups, forums, and virtual events.

5. Attend Events and Workshops

Attending conferences, workshops, or school fairs is an excellent opportunity for networking with people with similar interests and aspirations. Learn how to make the most of these events, from preparing questions to effective self-introduction. This section further discusses following up after events by keeping the connections alive.

6. Developing a "Personal Brand" to Attract Opportunities

Building a personal brand will help people know about your interests, values, and skills. Here is how you can build a personal brand as a young entrepreneur. You will see examples of what to put on your social media profiles, your websites, or your portfolios. You will then find out how it makes you more memorable to potential mentors and collaborators.

7. The Role of Peer Support

Sometimes, peers can be just as valuable as mentors. This chapter explains how developing a community of peers and partners creates a supportive context to foster individual growth and has people in their lives who will keep them accountable. Working together on projects as well as using each other as sounding boards for ideas, peer relationships can be a wellspring of motivation and creativity.

8. Maintaining and Expanding Relationships

Networking is not only making contact but staying in touch. This chapter provides suggestions for staying in touch with your network by frequently updating others, sharing great resources, and showing appreciation. You will find that consistency and true interest make up the foundation of long-lasting professional connections.

9. Dealing with Rejections and Building Resilience

Not every networking attempt will bear fruit. That's just part of the process, and it's perfectly fine. Handling rejection becomes the topic of this section. It is a reminder that even when you don't connect, that does not mean you won't see them or someone who will be interested in talking. Learn why it's necessary to continue attempting to connect and get to know your network of contacts.

You will discover that each attempt improves communication and confidence, bettering you for even greater things to come.

Summary Chapter

"Building a Network and Finding Mentors" points out that networking is a learnable skill to build that support system toward your entrepreneurial journey. Practical advice on reaching out to people, authentic connections, digital leverage, and mentoring will help you feel comfortable in forming connections meant to guide and inspire you. This chapter will show you that the basic idea of networking has less to do with age or experience and more about curiosity, respect, and genuine connection.

CHAPTER TEN

Failure and Learning from Failure

Learn how to meet the inevitable challenges that will come your way with Chapter 10, "Embracing Failure and Learning from Setbacks." Failure is not something to dread-it's an opportunity for you to learn, grow, and refine your efforts. You'll be shown how to help yourself both refract setbacks and learn mistakes, and use failure as a stepping stone towards ultimate success.

1. The Fear of Failure: Why It Holds You Back Fear of failure can be paralyzing. It holds especially so for teenagers, where expectations of success can run particularly high. Here we go into the psychology of fear and why it is part of the entrepreneurial journey. Learn how to identify and overcome fear and the fear of failure that "freezes" most from action and risk.

2. Changing Your Mindset: From Fear to Opportunity

Transformation of failure into an opportunity is dependent on perception. As long as failure is viewed as negative, the possibility of turning it into something positive is very low. This chapter will help you to become really good at changing your mindset from fear to an opportunity and possibility.

3. Famous Entrepreneurs Who Failed

Most successful entrepreneurs have had significant failures before they could achieve success. This article will tell you about Steve Jobs, Elon Musk, and Thomas Edison who all had setbacks but ended up using it as a stepping stone to their subsequent successes. These real-life examples help you in understanding that failure is most often a part of the way to greatness.

4. The Power of Perseverance and Resilience

Resilience is about bouncing back from setbacks, and one of the most critical things an entrepreneur must establish. The rest of this chapter describes how the talents of persistence and resilience will make you a more robust and effective entrepreneur. It divulges actual strategies on how you might cultivate resilience, such as setting small goals, celebrating in progress, and practicing self-compassion.

5. Learning from Mistakes: How To Turn Failures into Lessons

This chapter does not focus on what went wrong but how to learn from the errors. You will see how to break down what happened, what you would do differently and apply it to the next lesson. In this chapter, the ways of journaling and reflection will also be discussed in ways to track one's progress and growth.

6. Business Failures

You're going to fail at some point in entrepreneurship-whether it's a failed product launch, a marketing campaign that didn't work, or a partnership that fell through. This chapter guides you through some of the common business setbacks young entrepreneurs face and discusses strategies for how to get through them. Understand that each failure is a chance to hone your skills and tactics.

7. How to Use Feedback Productively

Improving is impossible without feedback, but you never like hearing that something you did was wrong because you feel passionately about your work. This chapter helps you understand how to receive positive feedback-that is difficult to listen to-most constructively. You will discover how to use positive and negative feedback in such a way as to improve your products and services and for personal development.

8. The Critical Role of Risk-Taking and Experimentation

Entrepreneurship is risky by nature, but it's not mindless risk-taking-it's also smart risk-taking and lots of experimenting with new ideas. Here, you'll find the need to leave your comfort zones behind and explore new things that might just not work. You'll learn that the most significant success sometimes happens because of taking bold, well-informed risks and embracing the lessons learned from experimentation.

9. After a Personal Failure:

Sometimes, failure is not just professional but also personal. Balancing schoolwork and your business, handling social pressures, or dealing with personal doubts will eventually bring setbacks in all of these areas. In this section, you'll learn how to deal with personal challenges and stay motivated in the face of emotional and social obstacles. Do not forget that personal setbacks are equally important to work through as those in your business, and they are key learning opportunities in resilience and self-awareness.

10. Taking Failure as a Motivator to Success

This chapter ties everything together as you would show how you might use failure as a strong motivator. Instead of becoming a victim of your failures in the past, you will learn how to use them as fuel for your future investments. You will realize every time you get up from a fall that you are better prepared to take on the next challenge.

Chapter Summary:

In "Embracing Failure and Learning from Setbacks," you will learn how to transform failure as an integral component of the entrepreneurial process. With practical application of mindset shifts, learning from failure, and building resilience, this chapter helps you step into challenges directly head-on. Through the stories of famous entrepreneurs, tangible strategies, and personal reflection, failure isn't something to be avoided-but rather, a necessary step toward success. By the end of

CHAPTER ELEVEN

ACTION AND MOVING FORWARD WITH CONFIDENCE

We have seen the last chapter, "Taking Action and Moving Forward with Confidence," as an umbrella of everything learned in the book to develop a roadmap for turning ideas into action. It is an effort to step into that new life and business you have always dreamt of, with the knowledge, mindset, and skills developed until now. It talks about procrastination, clear goal-setting, and how to build confident momentum.

1. Get Out of Procrastination: How to Get Moving Today

It is one of the biggest obstacles that a young person with big dreams faces. In this section, you will learn about the causes of procrastination as well as strategies on how to overcome it. You will come to understand why it is sometimes necessary to start small and how a small action today can be a step to greater gains in the following years. With practical tips on deadlines, breaking tasks into smaller steps, and sustaining accountability, you'll be ready to move from planning to action.

2. The Art of Goal Setting: From the Ideal to the Actionable Goal

A plan is just a wish without a dream. You shall learn, in this chapter, the need for definite, yet achievable goals, and how to break up those objectives into smaller actionable steps. You shall be introduced to the SMART goal framework-Specific, Measurable, Achievable, Relevant, Time-bound-and how it may be used in making a roadmap toward entrepreneurial endeavor. Lastly, you shall learn the importance of monitoring progress and necessary adjustment based on results.

Chapter 3 : Building Momentum: From Small Seeds, Big Plans Momentum is what helps sustain motivation and succeed over the long term. You will discover in this chapter how starting from small acorn-sized seedlings can be a snowball effect: each little victory builds your confidence to propel you toward larger and larger goals. Learn how to embrace and celebrate your small wins and how such feelings of progress will energize and keep you moving forward.

4. Developing Confidence Trust in Self and Ability

In confidence, the way forward in any entrepreneurship venture is built. This section shall guide you on how to build your self-confidence: building your skills and finding the right people. You find that confidence is not about being perfect but about trusting your ability to learn and grow. Advice in action includes affirmations, visualized performances, and learning from others who have done it.

5. It's Living the Process: In joy; for the love of the doing, not just for the destination.

Entrepreneurship is a long and often grueling journey. This chapter reminds you that success is not a destination-it's a process, too. You will learn how to find pleasure in the ups and downs of the entrepreneurial experience as well as fulfillment in the journey itself. Focus on continuous learning, growth, problem-solving, and embedding joy into the very processes of creating and building something meaningful.

6. Learning to Prioritize: Understanding How to Manage Your Time as a Means of Focusing on What Truly Matters

Being a young entrepreneur is likely to draw you into a boomerang between school and social life and then your business at the same time. Thus, in this section, you'll learn how to prioritize the right tasks to effectively time-management. You'll get techniques on how to stay organized and set boundaries on the important things that will help bring you closer to your goals. Tools and tips on time management will be shared so that you can keep ahead of both your business and your academic commitments.

7. Building Your Support System: Surrounding Yourself with the Right People One of the greatest things that you can have is a great support system. You will learn how to surround yourself with individuals who believe in your dreams and people who will encourage and mentor you along the way. Whether it's family, friends, or fellow entrepreneurs, building relationships with the right people is crucial to your success. You will also learn how to find mentors and professional networks of other young entrepreneurs who can share their experiences and insights.

8. Conquering Skepticism: How to Deal with Self-Doubt and External Detractors

Somewhere along the line, you will start doubting-yourself and others will doubt you too. This chapter is here to help you know that it's normal and that it will not mean you have to be held back. You will find out how to manage negative self-talk, how to overcome external criticism, and how to keep your eyes on the vision by the end of this chapter. Some practical tips to reframe negative thoughts, looking for constructive criticism, and using doubt to fuel your desire to prove them wrong.

9. Consistency: How to Create Habits for Success

More often than not, consistency is the real difference between making it and not. In this chapter, you'll find out how daily habits are powerful and how consistent routines lead to long-term achievement - whether that's setting aside thirty minutes every day to work on your business, getting exercised daily, or even just time to grow as a person, because small daily actions stack up to create huge results. You'll know how to build habits that will support your goals and keep you going when things get tough.

10. Staying Committed: How to Keep Going Even When You Face Challenges

The last part of this book speaks about perseverance. Entrepreneurship has many ups and downs, but the rule for success is to stay the course even when you don't feel like you're gaining much ground. You will be inspired to press forward, no matter what gets thrown your way, and to know that every challenge you face and conquer makes you tougher and stronger. Persistence, with a positive attitude, will be your best friend on your journey to achieving success.

Summary of the Chapter

This chapter, "Taking Action and Moving Forward with Confidence," explains the steps to take into action that first, crucial step to the realization of entrepreneurial dreams. Overcoming procrastination and how to set actionable goals and become confident through commitment-this chapter outlines the action plan for moving forward with determination and clarity. By the end of this chapter, you will have a clear plan of action and the confidence to pursue your dreams with unstoppable momentum. It could be your business, it could be personal growth, or anything else you want to do. You will come to know how to move forward regardless of what life throws your way.

Well, Now It Is Your Turn - Do Not Wait, Act!

As we close on this journey together now, it is time to reflect on all that you have learned and how you are to apply it. "Now or Never" was much more about challenging you to think big or dream big as it would be about empowering you to take immediate steps toward making those dreams a reality.

You learned that it's not the age that limits you but rather it's an advantage. You found that, with the right mindset, resources, and actions, there's no need why you cannot start building your future today. How to defeat fear and procrastination; ability to set goals, learn from failure, surround people who can guide you through this process.

The most important one of all, though is this: if there is something in your way, and your goal, it is the action now. You think each and every one of those successful persons you want to be waited until they felt "ready." You think that they waited for things to be perfect. They simply started taking action, and so can you.

The bottom line is, there is always now to start.

And at the end of it all, this issue does not boil down to how old you are or even how much experience you have. It simply boils down to showing enough guts to take that first step forward and sticking through it no matter what comes next.

And armed with that knowledge, tool that you need and at the right mindset, the hour has come. Your future is there, and those opportunities that you have always wished for are waiting for you. Don't let a minute more pass, nor another day go by without doing what you want to do, for your time has come.

I believe in you. And then, you take everything that you learn, and you put it into practice-then there's no other way for you to be able to fail.

You are the future-and the future is now.

Conclusion & Portfolio

Thank you for joining me on this journey through Now or Never. My goal is to inspire and equip young entrepreneurs with the mindset and strategies to turn their dreams into reality. Remember, success isn't about age—it's about taking action.

About the Author – Shravan Narayan

• Founder & CEO of Code Cave – A leading IT company with 500+ successful projects across the UK, UAE, Qatar, and more, generated six-figure revenue.

• CO-Founder & CEO of My Ward – A tech-driven initiative under Talrop, revolutionizing governance through digital solutions.

• CO-Founder & CEO of Chaseplus Learning – Empowering students with career guidance, AI, and tech awareness.

• Master Tutor at Steyp – A software engineering edtech platform, mentoring young minds in technology and innovation.

• Startup Mentor – Supporting and guiding emerging entrepreneurs.

Achievements:

• Entrepreneurship Award – Talrop-Reporter Technology Conference.

• 100+ sessions on career guidance, AI, and technology across various platforms.

• Multiple Hackathon Wins – Recognized in Bangalore, Kochi, and beyond.

• Featured in Leading Media Outlets – Highlighted for contributions to tech and entrepreneurship.

• Dream Achiever – Turning visions into reality with dedication and innovation.

• Won Robotics Competitions – Showcasing expertise in AI, automation, and robotics innovation.

This is just the beginning. I'm actively involved in upcoming startups, innovations, and business ventures. Let's connect and build the future together!

Get in Touch:

Email: shravannarayan.official@gmail.com

Instagram: @shravan_narayan

LinkedIn: www.linkedin.com/in/shravannarayan